Ex Libris

A Treasury
of Design
Ideas for
Your Home

Raymond Waites

SMALL PLEASURES

Photographs by
Tom McCavera
Charles Maraia
Cole Riggs

A Bulfinch Press Book   Little, Brown and Company   Boston • Toronto • London

*My special feelings
to my wife,
Nancy Candler Waites,
whose magical eyes
and whimsical heart
have developed
my talents and
given*

A Visual Scrapbook of Design Ideas, Personal Thoughts, & Golden Memories.

My special thanks to Geoffrey Bradfield,
for his introduction to Lindley Boegehold, my editor at Bulfinch Press/Little, Brown.

My thanks to RitaSue Siegel, my agent,
for her belief in me through the years and diligence throughout this project.

My thanks to Armstrong World Industries, Inc.,
for selecting me to design many of the wonderful interiors used in this book.

My thanks to Bruce Bordelon, my lawyer,
for his advice and for making my homes a reality, without which this book would not be possible.

McCavera

Raymond Waites

SMALL PLEASURES

*To
Armi
&
Ristomatti
Ratia
for
Golden
Memories.*

At Bökars I remember candlelight. It came from an odd assortment of chandeliers Armi Ratia had collected in her travels and hung over a big round table. The perfect setting for fantasy.

*L*ife is a mosaic of small moments and of visual treats experienced in a second; like the silhouette of a flower against a patterned wall. There are also moments that involve all the senses—taste, touch, smell, sound, and sight. Think about the fragrance of fresh flowers, the warm touch of wood, the crisp feel of linen. These small pleasures bring beauty into our lives. You can start with one of these ideas and build on it. Linked together, such small pleasures add up to a total life experience.

During one of these moments as I thought about this book, I looked through my photographs and walked around my home. The idea of a scrapbook—showing bits and pieces of my life and work, shared with my wife Nancy and our friends—began to take form. Some of the photographs are only snapshots, but they evoke a feeling or bring back a memory. Too often, we let our lack of technical knowledge make us afraid to try something. It shouldn't.

*D*esign, creativity, and love of home are fun and essential in my life. Nancy and I met at Auburn University in Alabama. Nancy is from an old Southern family that founded Agnes Scott College and the Coca-Cola Company in Atlanta. I am from the small village of Demopolis, Alabama. We fell in love and we moved to New York on my fellowship grant to study design at Pratt Institute in New York.

On our first day in New York, we walked into the Design Research shop, then on East 57th Street, to buy a bed. This was our introduction to a whole new world and way of living. We were immediately captivated. Within days, Nancy was working for DR, as it was called. Marimekko, a brand of fabric they featured, gave a generation of Americans a new way to look at living spaces. The furniture was clean and contemporary, and architecture was its soul. The fabrics and clothing were bold, bright, strong, and full of life. We were in love.

*A*rmi Ratia, the magical Finnish woman who created the Marimekko vision, was to become the strongest creative force in my life. DR became a home away from home for an international group. One member, Helja Burgon, knew Armi, having worked in Finland at the Marimekko headquarters. She insisted we invite Armi to see what she called the "Marimekko-land" we had created in our Brooklyn Heights apartment. Armi accepted our invitation. Her work had been featured in *Life, Elle,* and *Mobilia,* but we figured she'd never had a real Southern down-home dinner and evening. Overnight, what started as a small, intimate meal for 6 became dinner for 30. Like madmen, Nancy and I began frying chicken, making pecan pies, and stewing collard greens. One of my best memories is my first sight of Armi and Ristomatti, her son, climbing the stairs to our top-floor apartment, arms filled with enormous bouquets of white roses.

It was a magical night, the start of a great adventure that changed my life and developed my eyes, introducing me to a world of creativity, great heart, fantasy, and vision. Armi and Risto became my mentors. They showed me that everything is possible, that a simple thing, done with a grand gesture, can be very special.

Later I spent a wonderful evening in Finland at Bökars, Armi's country house on the Baltic. When I close my eyes and think of that enchanting evening, I remember the warmth of the candlelight.

Guests at Bökars were the president of DR, a delightfully mad French woman from the fashion industry, a Finnish ballerina, someone who lived in a windmill on the property, and Risto. Armi raised her glass of vodka for the first toast and said, "Let's get up and in five minutes come back in costume made from things you find around the house." Only at Armi's would there be no question that this was something one did with great gusto. In five minutes we returned in Felliniesque apparel, the ballerina in a marvelous dress made from a lace coverlet, the president wrapped like a Viking in a fur rug, Armi layered in her collection of Moroccan jewelry, and the staff with baskets tied on their heads, pouring wine. Armi could make any dinner an adventure.

Armi's city apartment was minimalist and cool. Her country house was warm, comfortable, and friendly, the ideal backdrop for fantasy and the perfect place to relax.

Each bedroom was decorated differently. Some were simple and restrained, in the style of the time. To my surprise, I always chose the bedroom with red walls. It was a magical room, with Victorian furniture and a crazy gold cupid hanging over the bed.

I discovered two sides of my creative soul in Finland—the simple, clean design side and the robust, decorative one.

Armi taught me how to use these expressive pieces of our past as she had used elements of her Finnish tradition at Bökars—not in an intimidating, formal historical way, but by using the furniture, fabric, wallpaper, and decorative objects as a painter uses paint on a palette, to layer a room with color, texture, mood, emotion, and life.

I want to show you how to look around you to find these bits and pieces of your life and how to use them in unique and inventive ways. Don't be afraid of your friends coming into your home and saying, "You're crazy." This book will help you say, "I can do it!" It's about capturing memories, about sharing, about fantasy, and above all, it's about having fun.

Armi's Country Baroque bedroom was the room I chose each weekend with its red walls and Victorian furniture covered in an unexpected wave of Marimekko color in red and black. There was a large floor-to-ceiling gold-leaf mirror, very reminiscent of entryway mirrors in Southern homes. And hanging above the bed was this crazy gold cupid, exactly the "wrong" thing to do, but it was magic.

As I look to the future, I see a new design energy evolving. The 1930s gave birth to a design aesthetic that was rich and elegant in contrast to a time of financial instability. In the same way, the design of interiors in these chaotic times is taking on a new mood of elegance and opulence.

Over the past few years, many Americans have become educated about good design. Interiors and fashion have both had an exuberant renaissance. Americans have been exposed to a harvest of books and magazines, which have educated their eyes.

The 1980s was the age of country design and country charm. The blue-jean generation adopted the rustic and casual. Easy-to-understand miniprints, soft grayed colors, and, of course, American folk art were new to us and mirrored the decade.

Today, the key words for our homes are casual elegance. People are responding to precious things used in a relaxed, casual way. Design is traditional in feeling, but not stuffy. I'll show you the new ways to deal with traditional elements: rich materials, spice tones, gold, baroque style, seventeenth- and eighteenth-century art.

The new key design styles for the 1990s are Country Classic, Neo-Classical, Neo-Traditional, and Country Baroque. In this book I'm showing groups of design ideas that bring color, pattern, and textures together in ways that are familiar and comfortable, but refreshing and unexpected, creating a tension between the old and the new.

The 1960s was a time of both unrest and inventiveness. Marimekko was at the forefront of this burst of invention. Its colors were bright, new, and outrageous. Hot pink! Purple! Daffodil yellow! It was exciting and it fit the youth-oriented culture of the time.

As we moved through the 1970s, Americans looked inward as we celebrated the bicentennial. Brimfield, Rhinebeck, and the Hamptons antique fairs became major cultural events capturing national attention. They changed our eye.

*T*he Biennale Show in Paris was a blaze of exuberant red color and rich patterns, Baroque scrolls, garlands and flowers, faux leopard prints. The new styles shown were Neo-Traditional, Neo-Classical, Neo-Baroque, Neo-Renaissance, and Neo-Modern.

A visual scrap-book of antique fabrics, nineteenth-century painted designs, and novelty cards. They are great collectibles and still a good value.

Right after the bicentennial, in 1977, I left Finland and returned to America. Home again, I fell in love with country pine and bits and pieces of quilts. I was charmed by the imperfect world of country living. It was full of warmth, it was welcoming, and it had great heart.

That year, I bought my first piece of pine furniture, a wonderful eighteenth-century folk art piece from Vermont. I translated this personal interest into my professional design life in 1978, by creating Gear Design and Marketing, with Bettye Martin and her husband, Bill Musham. It was no coincidence that *Country Living* Magazine was founded in the same year.

The new colors that I began to work with in my country collections were very different from the bold and bright colors of the '60s and early '70s. They were colors from nature. I designed my first wallpaper and fabric book in 1980, *American Country*, a collection of mini prints in soft, country colors.

When I started working with many different manufacturers in America to create a coordinated color palette for the American Country collection, I was astounded to find that the companies never communicated with one another. You couldn't get a wallpaper to match a sheet, or a shower curtain that went with a towel. Today that's all changed. There has been a design explosion.

As we approach the millennium, we are moving into a new design stage. We've learned how to use simpler design and are beginning to explore more decorative arts. The photographs in this part of the book were taken at the Biennale Show, which is a major trend-setting decorative arts show held every two years in Paris. Overall, this new feeling that is evolving conveys substance and timelessness; it is a feeling of yesterday used with a very modern attitude. Gone are the rooms to be only looked at; these are rooms to be lived in and enjoyed. They are rooms of fantasy, rooms of great colors, fabrics, and wonderful moods.

Our collection of nineteenth-century decorative steel engravings, textile paintings, accessories, and jewelry in a harvest of green, creating a world of wildlife treasures.

The wildlife mood enveloped the Biennale Show in Paris. Leaf motifs, all hues of green and gold, rich accents of nature, created a mood in harmony with our ecology-minded '90s.

$\mathcal{A}$ small design that creates the wildlife mood are these simple pin cushions that I created as Christmas gifts this year. Small in scale, only 8½ inches long by 6 inches wide, these are a small gift that will give pleasure each time you put your treasures in place for visual fun.

$\mathcal{C}$ollectibles are a harvest of antique pins from the antique fairs in the Hamptons. These were salesmen's samples, hence the intricate detail on such a small scale. The pin cushions are made by new friend Linda Bentson of Thief River Linen.

SMALL PLEASURES

In The Neo-Classical Style

A Scrapbook Of Ideas, Thoughts & Memories

Neo-Classic is timeless. Classical antiquity created a design vision so elegant that it inspires every age. The fascinations of classical design, the sensual materials, the visual rhythms, the sense of balance, remain the focus for imagination.

One of my earliest memories of textures, used in an expressive way was from a visit to Castle Rosenborg in Copenhagen. I was enthralled by the contrast created.

The rediscovery began in the late Renaissance with the architect Palladio, whose adaptations of Roman buildings inspired the vigorous Palladian style of the 1700s.

Later architects discovered other Neo-Classic idioms, sometimes simple, sometimes imaginatively detailed. The timeless elegance of this idiom leads to the intermittent reappearance of classical revivals, whether austere or ebullient. Our culture is always moving, design ideas ebb and flow. As we move towards the millennium, the Neo-Classical style has returned to favor.

Faux finishes, classical urns, marble, decoupage, all these effects are becoming an integral part of our interiors—We are picking up brush, sponge and template, or wallpaper to create marvelous textured effects in a Neo-Classical mood.

Faux Pleasures

Neo-Classic architectural urns used with an unexpected mix of objects creates your own Neo-Classic garden in your home.

In the florist and accessory shops are wonderful Hydrocal urns and classical architectural details in a wide variety of faux finishes. They allow you to create your own corner of antiquity. I love

to put together unexpected elements, a lustreware sphere combined with twig wreaths and large wooden hoops that have been gold-leafed in a crackle finish to create an unexpected change from the classic floral display. Spheres of marble and wire repeat the design theme.

Textures and faux finishes are two of the most beautiful and easy solutions for the walls, whether you paint them yourself, employ an artist reviving this ancient skill, or use the newest and easiest wallpapers with patterns that emulate hand technique. I've always loved the printing process and have specified printing techniques for my wallpapers that emulate the character of faux painted walls, whether faux marble, stria, stipples, or sponging.

Return to Renaissance

I found this painting of cupids in a flea market in Paris.
The search for collected treasures is joyful and entertaining. Never be afraid to ask the price,
sometimes you get a nice surprise.

Two years ago, a window full of attractive objects caught my eye. Inside were even more fascinating items. I turned to go, thinking everything was too expensive, but as I did, I asked the proprietor, "How much is the painting in the corner?" I was shocked at how inexpensive it was. The deal was made. I started falling in love with cupids. Several of my friends who are interior or fashion designers share this passion. Notice that cupids have begun to appear in important interiors in all the magazines. Here, I've hung this very special treasure on a faux marble wall with just a touch of metallic ribbon. As the seasons change, or even for special dinner parties, the ribbon may change color or may be replaced with a tassel. You should move your art around the house as you do other decorative objects. As the seasons change, as your moods change, change the art that surrounds you.

Ribbons, tassels, and ropings are elegant and beautiful elements to enrich your home. Add these decorative hanging details as shown in the photograph.

Masterful Mix

The floral arrangements I enjoy most use both natural and faux elements.
Most of the flowers in this bouquet were simply left out to dry. Shops springing up all over the country
stock an incredible array of dried flowers, weeds, and vegetables. The choice is endless.

Mixing elements is an exciting way to add interest to something you do every day. In this luxurious arrangement a bit of plastic ivy takes on a new life in its natural habitat.

The container is all important in creating this Neo-Classical presentation. Here I have used a cast iron urn, painted in the classical black finish.

Materials:
1. Newspaper
2. Plastic floral or ivy leaves
3. Gold spray paint
4. Dried hydrangeas, dried pomegranates and artichokes, bittersweet, or many other combination of dried flowers and fruit
5. A large urn or vase

Step 1. Cover your work area with newspaper to protect other objects from overspray. Lay the plastic leaves on the paper and spray with gold paint.
Step 2. Arrange the dried hydrangeas, fruits, and vegetables in the urn.
Step 3. When the plastic leaves have dried, insert them among the dried arrangement.

The landscape is enhanced by the addition of a marble sphere and a wonderful baroque piece of pressed metal. Originally designed as a curtain back, I simply rolled it into a large cuff which Nancy wore as a bracelet to the costume show at the Metropolitan Museum of Art.

A Playful Hand

To create visual moments, I group similar shapes that have contrasting finishes and patterns.

I play endlessly with new ways to group the things I love.

Materials:

1. Wood or plastic spheres
2. Silver spray paint
3. Pearlized paints in assorted colors
4. Elmer's Glue-All
5. Assorted small brushes
6. Dragées (cake decorations)
7. Glass with a diameter less than the width of the sphere
8. Pencil
9. Tray or pie plate to hold the glass
10. Bowl for glue

Step 1. Paint both spheres, one in silver, one in pearlized ivory.

Step 2. Put glue in a bowl. Roll or brush Elmer's Glue-All onto one half of the silver sphere. Use glue at full strength. Roll in or toss dragées over sphere on the tray to catch falling dragées. It will be difficult to cover the entire sphere as the dragées have a tendency to fall off. The accidental quality of the irregular placement is beautiful. The glue at this stage is a milky white, but when it dries, it should give a clear, soft matte finish to your sphere.

Step 3. Place on glass to dry.

Step 4. When dry, repeat for other half.

Step 5. Repeat same procedure for remainder of spheres.

Step 6. Mix your paints to create a green pearl, copper pearl, and red pearl.

Step 7. With a light pencil, draw a baroque vine swirl pattern over sphere.

Step 8. First paint the vine copper, creating the swirl that the leaves and berries will be added to.

Step 9. Add the leaves and berries to the vine design in green and red pearl paint. Do not be afraid if your leaves and berries have an irregular quality. It is all part of the hand-painted folk art look of this wonderful pearlized ornament.

Collectibles: a nineteenth century English horn and silver tumbler. Black Shoulders ceramic egg with bunny detail from Tiffany's. Italian enamelled-on-silver Fabergé-style decorative egg. Stone etched egg with white speckles from En- Pottery in East Hampton, New York. dpainted box from the Tower of Lon- Pedestal in cinnabar color from Vic- tiques, New York City, a reproduc- of molded stone. To the left, nineteenth-century cameos rest in a flea market find washed in a coat of gold.

Many of my friends share my passion for creating decorative objects. Jean Marie Nols and Lee Stout make these elegant architectural spheres from nuts of all varieties.

These are elegantly simple in their geometry yet visually intricate when used together in an architectural landscape.

Materials:
1. Styrofoam sphere, choice of size
2. Masking tape
3. Hot glue gun
4. Nuts of all varieties. Here we show pistachios, hazelnuts, walnuts
5. Spanish moss
6. Small knife for inserting the moss between the nuts

Step 1. Cover the sphere with masking tape, as the hot glue would melt the styrofoam.

Step 2. Glue the nuts in place, covering the entire sphere.

Step 3. With the knife, press pieces of the moss between the nuts to cover up the masking tape and hot glue.

Collectibles are marble pyramids, golden wire ornaments, and a faux painted chest from the antique fair in Bridgehampton.

Grand Illusions

A farm table becomes a Neo-Classical fantasy when painted, spattered and decoupaged. New and used pieces of furniture can be used to equal effect.

Dressing up a discarded table, chest or chair can give it new life and personality. The combination of simple sponge techniques, spatter painting and gluing of steel engravings on furniture creates a family heirloom to be passed down from generation to generation.

Materials
1. Sandpaper
2. Acrylic paint in white, raw umber and black
3. Flat dishes
4. Natural sponge
5. White test paper
6. Assorted paint brushes
7. Gold paint
8. Xeroxes of chosen steel engravings
9. Scissors
10. Elmer's Glue-All
11. Spray varnish; clear, semi-gloss
12. Flour
13. Soft cloth

Step 1. Clean all surfaces of table. Lightly sandpaper top of piece of furniture. Don't worry about imperfections.
Step 2. Mix white paint with a small amount of black to create a light grey color. Paint top of table. Let dry.
Step 3. In a flat dish, mix white and black

acrylic paint with a dash of raw umber to create a darker value of grey. Mix a small amount to the consistency of heavy cream.
Step 4. Dip sponge into pan and test on white paper to see what kind of texture your sponge gives, then freely sponge entire top of table in an irregular pattern.
Step 5. Mix white, raw umber and black paint to create another lighter shade of color and repeat Step 4.
Step 6. Mix a small amount of black with the raw umber and white to create a grey/brown color of medium value. With a small brush, draw irregular veins randomly across the top of the table.
Step 7. While still wet, whisk a dry stiff brush back and forth across these veins to soften and blur their edges. This should take at least 3–4 strokes over each vein.

Step 8. Add more veining in darker and lighter value if you want a more intricate effect.
Step 9. Paint edge of table as shown in photograph with gold paint as well as details in legs, as shown, if desired.
Step 10. With a large, hard, stiff brush, spatter top, edge and legs of table with two values of gray, one lighter and one darker, to create a spatter effect.
Step 11. From books or magazines make black and white Xeroxes of steel engravings, enough to create a tossed pattern across top of table. You will be surprised at how often they are used as illustrative elements. Invent your own pictorial story. If you love fruit or floral motifs, create a garden; architectural elements are also very dramatic.
Step 12. Cut out illustration to include rule line framing the image.
Step 13. With Elmer's Glue-All, adhere Xeroxes to painted tabletop. Let dry.
Step 14. With a medium value of grey paint, lightly spatter over entire top, including engravings.
Step 15. Spray with semi-gloss varnish. When varnish is almost dry, sprinkle with household flour and polish with a soft cloth. This will add a soft sheen to the finished creation.

Portrait in Needlepoint

*Years ago, Nancy's mother asked if she could needlepoint a
design for us. To her surprise, I designed a self portrait in needlepoint.*

In our apartment, this black-and-white pillow is a wonderful bit of graphic humor. This idea is also wonderful for a child's room in ivory and baby blue or soft rose.

Materials:
1. A clear black and white or color photograph of someone you love
2. Three pencils, #1, 2, and 3
3. Masking tape
4. Needles to fit the yarn size
5. Needlepoint canvas, your choice of size
6. Black and white yarn
7. Black or white canvas fabric for backing

Step 1. Try to select a photo that has strong side lighting and picks up the details of the facial features for best effect. Xerox and enlarge your photograph to size desired. Work with the contrast on the Xerox machine to render the photographic image primarily in black and white, with no grey tones. This can be done by repeatedly Xeroxing the same image as you enlarge it. You will notice the line quality becomes grainy. This makes interesting detail for the finished pillow.

Step 2. After the image is the desired size, use a soft pencil, at least #2, to layer a heavy coat of graphite on the back of the image. The outline of the image will be transferred in graphite from the back of the Xerox onto your needlepointing canvas.

Step 3. Lay the canvas on a flat surface. Hold it in place with masking tape. Position the Xerox over the canvas and tape it on the top to hold it in place as you transfer the image. With a hard #1 pencil, trace the edges of your black-and-white design onto the canvas. Do not worry about getting every detail. Your image will create a graphic caricature as shown in the photograph, not a full-tone photographic effect. Once the outline is transferred to the canvas, shade in areas that contrast to make it easier when you begin your needlepointing.

Step 4. Needlepoint your design in the traditional "needlepoint" or "half cross" stitch. This stitch is easy and quick to work. Using the canvas, create 45⁰ angles as shown in photo.

Step 5. Back your pillow with white or black canvas. I suggest a zipper-style pillow case that can be removed when washed.

This display wall that I created is an ever-changing scrapbook. It is a wonderful way to enjoy our collectibles and can be re-designed for each special occasion. Here the table has been layered with a swirl of gold fabrics. The centerpiece of silk roses, dried hydrangeas, antique silver fruit, bits of antique lace, and a flourish of tulle adds a grand height to the buffet table. All you need as a base is a country basket wired atop a candlestick with florist's wire.

Decoupage Details

Wallpaper borders and stencilling for design interest have become a part of our homes in America. An old technique for wall covering that has been ignored until today is decoupage.

My first encounter with decoupage was when my Aunt Ruby and her friends began decoupaging their handbags during the '50s. It became quite the thing to do with Southern ladies' groups in Macon, Georgia. Today, decoupage has recaptured the interest of interior designers. Shown here is a detail that I added to my wall of collections.

Materials:
1. #2 Lead pencil.
2. 12″ Ruler.
3. Scissors.
4. Varied-texture patterned wallpapers in different colors (one roll of each should be enough unless you are planning a major undertaking. I used three textures of different colors to create the effect in the photograph.)
5. 1″ Wallpaper brush.
6. Wallpaper paste.
7. Sponge.
8. Satin or glossy varnish.

Step 1. With pencil, lightly draw the outer square of design shown directly on the wall.

Step 2. Measure dimensions of the square. With scissors cut red paper to the size of the square.

Step 3. Apply paste to the back of the red texture and position square within outline on wall.

Step 4. Cut four ¼″ strips of dark black texture and ½″ of grey. Apply strips of grey texture around red texture square. Mitre edges as you paste. Repeat this process for thin black ¼″ strips as shown. Mitre them on top of the ½″ grey strips. Be sure outer edge of black covers all of the red texture underneath to create a clean black edge. Do not worry about paste overflow. Brush paste freely as you apply strips; it can be easily removed in final clean up.

Step 5. Cut a small square from grey or black texture. The dimension of the square shown is 1¼″ but can be any size to fit your design.

Step 6. Center in red square as shown.

Step 7. Clean surface with lightly moistened sponge.

Step 8. Let dry overnight. If any edges curl, stick down with a small amount of Elmer's Glue-All. Varnish with a satin or glossy varnish as desired for a glazed or unglazed look. Don't be intimidated and try for perfection. In today's world of machine perfection, the imperfections of the human artist are part of the beauty of decoupage.

From the patterns of Venetian floors came the inspiration for my decoupage wall. Create your own inlay design for your home.

Civil War Remembrances

*A family heirloom that Nancy and I cherish is a Confederate bill
that Nancy's great-great-grandfather signed at the end of the conflict.*

A simple way to preserve historical artifacts such as this Confederate bill, a swatch of fabric, antique lace, or Victorian cards is to seal them between two sheets of glass. In this case, it was important to see both sides of the bill.

Materials:
1. Two sheets of glass, size chosen to fit your artifacts. (Glass treated with Ultra-violet is best.)
2. Masking tape.
3. Ribbon. Here I used gold metallic ribbon and a gold bullion ornament.
4. 100% Silicon rubber clear adhesive.

Step 1: Place artifacts between two sheets of clean glass.
Step 2: Seal edges on all four sides with masking tape. Be sure all edges are covered to create an airtight seal so dust will not be able to get inside.
Step 3: Glue ribbon on edge to cover tape. I turned the corners by simply knotting the ribbon, which created a 45-degree turn.

Assembled Treasures

This corner of family portraits and table pleasures evokes the dignified retreat of a Victorian gentleman.

The simplest of objects take on grand decorative presence when positioned and displayed on a classic candlestick. In the spirit of the Russian Tea Room in New York, which is year-round decked with Christmas decorations, I use many of our Christmas ornaments for special occasions in other seasons. Simple ideas: a cupid sitting atop a pedestal or a sphere atop a candlestick are wonderful additions to a dinner party as a centerpiece or a sideboard display.

Family treasures passed down over generations add heritage to your home. Nancy's grandmother, on a sojourn to Italy, had this wonderful painting of her grandfather George Washington Scott, executed on ivory and framed in this unique, carved ivory frame. To the left are two portraits of Nancy's great-grandfather and grandfather, portraits painted in the classic Victorian style from photographs. We have found some of our favorite paintings at an antique shop in Bridgehampton. This one was discovered last summer and framed in a deep cuff of gold with an interliner of intricate wood inlay.

Puppy Memorabilia

*Nancy loves dogs, especially our schnauzer, Boscha. From flea
markets and antique shops, she has assembled a collection of dog memorabilia in all shapes and sizes.*

Victorian decorative art reflects the nineteenth century English and American gentry's love of dogs. Below, man's best friend is commemorated on humorous brushes with ceramic dog heads that were used to whisk a gentleman's clothes. From the early 1900's, men's tie clasps and stick pins are dog portraits under glass. Silver matchbox covers depicting the Boston bull terrier, Victorian lead toys, steel engravings, metal embossed pins, costume jewelry Scotties with heads that move and a novelty card with a Beagle dressed up in a sailor suit, attest to Nancy's passion. My favorite is a folk art coin purse painted as a portrait of a Pointer. I use this at times as a wall hanging to hold dried flowers.

Nancy has named the wire-haired terrier on the pillow Xerxes. He was brought home from a shop on Portobello Road in London and only became an American citizen recently. This rug has been hooked in the classic hooking technique on velvet.

Try your hand at creating a needlepoint portrait of your pet. Use the technique described on page 46.

56

SMALL PLEASURES

In The

Country Baroque

Style

A Scrapbook Of Ideas, Thoughts & Memories

The Country Baroque style is grounded in contrast. This newly evolved country style is fun and playful, using nature's bounty and baroque treasures from American antique fairs and European shops.

Nature's bounty overflows from this elegant garden urn. Grapes, apples, limes, pineapples, mushrooms, and ivy cascade to make this Country Baroque display.

This slightly irreverent use of historical artifacts and decorative design ideas could only happen in our times. Both true antiquities and reproduced design elements are readily available for our use in whimsical or grand ways all year long.

Through the winter our home glows with golden candlelight. With the burst of spring, the flowers, the light, nature's bounty is outside our East Hampton windows. The touch is lighter, the green color of nature explodes around us. It sets the tone for summer joy, fun, and entertaining.

This maid's bench in Finland became a bed, to take advantage of sleeping in front of the stove on cold Scandinavian winter nights. In East Hampton the front wooden section pulls out to make way for midsummer night's dreams, when we have a full house on a summer weekend. It is a perfect guest bed.

A tablescape of decorative small pleasures: a brown paper shade I gold-leafed in faux leopard print, inexpensive plaster cupids, gold-leafed and antiqued, and beaded fruit from the antique fairs that have been given a flourish of golden leaves. Aunt You Hoo's candelabra has been garnished with golden shells and terra-cotta angels. Other cherished collectibles are memories recalled: Morocco by the primitive Earthenware tea pitcher, England by the Staffordshire dog, and memories of good friends by their gift of a Japanese vase with its classic oriental representation of nature.

Artful Edges

Pillows in a room are like jewelry on a woman's gown. They add
that extra decorative element that can be refined, exciting and witty.

In today's casual world, rooms that are formal and rigid can be intimidating. Interesting and contrasting pillow play can help a room unbend. An unusual combination of materials offers a visual treat.

Materials
1. Quilted gold lamé fabric, yardage as needed
2. A simple rayon stripe fabric
3. A cotton leopard print fabric
4. Rope trim

Edge 1: Gold Lamé Pillow.
Step 1. Make ½ inch spaghetti straps from fabric by cutting strips of fabric to 4½ inches in length. Turn and hem edges and ends of straps.
Step 2. On one end of pillow, instead of inserting a zipper, sew a 3-inch wide panel of fabric inside of both sides of opening. This will cover the ends of the pillow when the straps are tied.
Step 3. When sewing these panels in place insert 4 spaghetti straps in the seam, evenly spaced. Sew the seam.
Step 4. Knot the straps as shown in photograph.

Edge 2: Striped Pillow. Note: Don't sew up the seam of this pillow until you are ready to insert your triangles.

Step 1. Cut 3″ wide strip of fabric. Turn down ¼ inch on each side. Iron to hold crease. Fold in half and align edges. Sew closed. Iron flat. This creates a 1¼ inch strip of fabric.
Step 2. Place strip horizontally on a flat surface. Measure 1½″ in from right edge and pin. With your right hand, fold the top edge of the fabric towards the pin at a 45 degree angle. Flatten seam.
Step 3. With your left hand, fold the long end of the strip towards the pin at a 45 degree angle to touch the flap created on the right side. This forms a triangle as shown in photograph.
Step 4. Trim left side ¼ inch below triangle. Create as many of these triangular elements as needed to edge your pillow.
Step 5. Insert triangles in seam. Pin in place. Then sew edges of pillow.

Edge 3: Leopard Pillow.
Step 1. Baste rope trim along the edge of the pillow.
Step 2. As you turn the corner simply knot rope trim as shown to add this special detail. When you have trimmed the entire pillow, tuck the end of the rope in and sew it shut.

Family Memories

*Family photographs and heirlooms bring warmth and a sense of
tradition and heritage to a home. Being surrounded by photographs of family members from bygone
days or last summer's fun can trigger wonderful memories.*

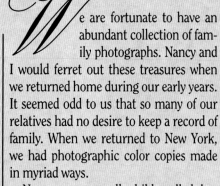

We are fortunate to have an abundant collection of family photographs. Nancy and I would ferret out these treasures when we returned home during our early years. It seemed odd to us that so many of our relatives had no desire to keep a record of family. When we returned to New York, we had photographic color copies made in myriad ways.

Nancy, as a small child, called her Great Aunt Nell Scott Candler "You Hoo." She would arrive each day at Nancy's house, open the door and call Yoo Hoo! From then on, all over Decatur, she was affectionately known as "You Hoo."

Nancy, her grandmother Izie and great aunt You Hoo are shown in these photographs, framed in nineteenth-century silver frames from one of our trips down Portobello Road in London. I added a decorative bow to each memory.

Inexpensive metal frames are given a touch of luxury with gilding.

68

A Golden Cornucopia

*Having to create just before guests arrive can sometimes bring
inventive results. One evening, I sprayed fresh pears with golden paint. I liked the idea so much that
I have incorporated it into many of my design projects over the years.*

In the 1950s, women began a new craft — beading fruits. You can now find examples in antique fairs everywhere. Over time, the beads have taken on an aged quality,

and material has gotten cloudy, developing a patina that gives the object a wonderful beauty. The leaves were always plastic. To soften and age this undesired surface, I antique and gold-leaf the foliage.

This cornucopia of fruits can be tossed simply in an urn or used as elements in the tablescapes to evoke the Country Baroque style.

Late nineteenth-century tapestry borders with leaf motifs were popular and used for bellpulls, pillows, and decorative trim.

Gilded Fancies

Gilded details have been added to a simple country pine piece to create a baroque fantasy.

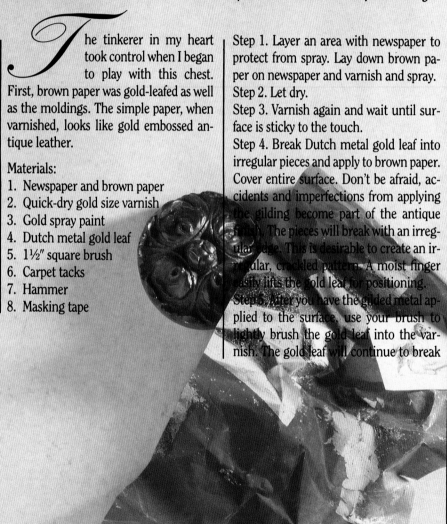

The tinkerer in my heart took control when I began to play with this chest. First, brown paper was gold-leafed as well as the moldings. The simple paper, when varnished, looks like gold embossed antique leather.

Materials:
1. Newspaper and brown paper
2. Quick-dry gold size varnish
3. Gold spray paint
4. Dutch metal gold leaf
5. 1½″ square brush
6. Carpet tacks
7. Hammer
8. Masking tape

Step 1. Layer an area with newspaper to protect from spray. Lay down brown paper on newspaper and varnish and spray.

Step 2. Let dry.

Step 3. Varnish again and wait until surface is sticky to the touch.

Step 4. Break Dutch metal gold leaf into irregular pieces and apply to brown paper. Cover entire surface. Don't be afraid, accidents and imperfections from applying the gilding become part of the antique finish. The pieces will break with an irregular edge. This is desirable to create an irregular, crackled pattern. A moist finger easily lifts the gold leaf for positioning.

Step 5. After you have the gilded metal applied to the surface, use your brush to lightly brush the gold leaf into the varnish. The gold leaf will continue to break

away and create an interesting speckled effect.

Step 6. Let surface dry. Lightly moisten a finger, handy cloth, or tissue with water and rub the surface to be sure all loose edges of gilt are rubbed into place.

Step 7. Crush paper into desired garland shape as shown in photo. It is easy to adjust and fold into desired shape.

Step 8. Tack paper in place.

To complete your own baroque fantasy, edge a piece of furniture with the same gold-leaf crackled finish as used on the brown paper above.

Step 9. Mask the piece so that only the desired surface to be gold-leafed is exposed. Newspaper edged with masking tape can be used to protect large areas from gold spray paint.

Step 10. Spray exposed area with gold paint. Let dry.

Step 11. Varnish exposed area. Let dry to tacky stage. Break gold leaf into small irregular pieces. Apply as you did before in the previous instructions.

Step 12. Remove masking tape right after you finish rubbing the surface. The longer it stays on, the harder it is to remove.

Glorious Bag

*What could be a simpler, faster wrap for a last-minute party gift
than a brown paper bag tied with a golden ribbon, garnished with a solar bookmark,
a rose, or golden fruit.*

This idea works throughout the year. I always keep a selection of various kinds of bags to wrap a dinner gift of wine or chocolates. Bags today come in an array of beautiful patterns, but easiest of all is a plain brown bag dressed up for party time. Whether trimmed with fresh roses,

tasseled, or tied with golden fruit, it's an instant giftwrap solution.

Collectibles include a nineteenth-century oval horn box with an insert of topaz. Modern soapstone bowl handcrafted and painted by the artist. Golden cupid and a family photo of Aunt You Hoo.

Brown Paper Glory

*Christmas gifts become an elegant play of everyday materials
when brown paper dressed up with gold and silver is used for wrapping
by my friends, Ben Formby and Michael McCardle.*

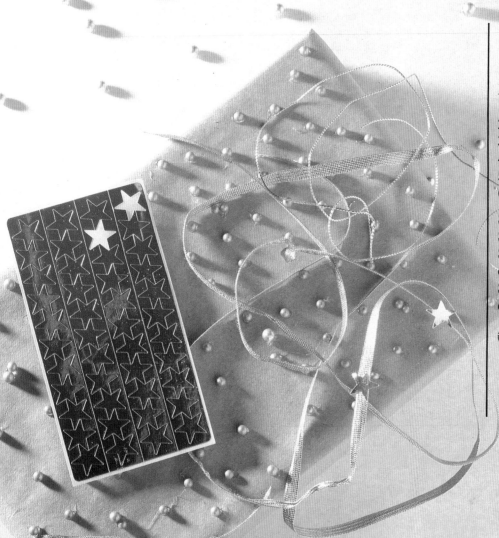

Wrapping packages creatively makes gift giving even more pleasurable.

Materials:
1. Brown paper
2. Scotch tape
3. Gold press-on stars
4. Hot glue gun
5. Dragées in gold and silver
6. Gold and silver ribbons

Step 1. Wrap packages with brown paper.
Step 2. Apply gold press-on stars.
Step 3. Hot-glue gold and silver dragées over package as shown.
Step 4. Trim with gold and silver ribbons of choice.

Baroque Splendor

*Velvet artichokes perched upon a column of silver
evoke a baroque garden harvest.*

My fascination with fruits and vegetables helped to create an elegant everlasting topiary. This historic art has been enthusiastically revisited by designers and gardeners in the last few years. From beautiful, dried roses to balls of ivy, we have fallen in love with this elegant garden form in miniature. You can easily create an artichoke with simple velvet leaves and dew drops of pearls.

Materials:
1. Styrofoam ball, your choice of size
2. Drinking glass, with a rim slightly smaller than the diameter of the ball to hold ball while working
3. Pearl corsage pins
4. Scissors
5. Velvet leaves from your florist's shop
6. Ribbon

Step 1. For easier working, position ball on drinking glass.
Step 2. Position a pearl pin in the ball to create the starting point of the design.
Step 3. Cut stems of velvet leaves to approximately ½" in length.
Step 4. Fold stems at 45-degree angle to the leaf.

Step 5. At pearl pin, which marks the top of the artichoke bloom, begin by positioning four leaves in north, south, east, west directions with the point of each leaf towards the pin. Press the stems into the foam ball. With this north, south, east, west orientation, work velvet leaves from this point of the blossom towards the stem end of the ball. Once these four quadrants are established, fill in the spaces between the leaves with evenly spaced overlapping leaves to cover Styrofoam ball completely, as shown in photograph.
Step 6. After leaves cover entire sphere, add a ribbon bow at the base of the artichoke blossom and secure with pearl pin.
Step 7. Where the leaves intersect insert a pearl corsage pin as shown. This not only adds a beautiful decorative detail, but holds leaves securely in place.

Together, the glow of candlelight and this elegant topiary add a baroque mood to buffet tables, sideboards, or entrance hall displays. Bowls or baskets of these decorative artichokes also can be used as centerpieces.

Topiary Treasures

A small Victorian garden is created by garnishing this topiary of velvet leaves with Nancy's collection of Victorian jewelry.

A wonderful topiary can be created using a found twig and a discarded terra cotta pot painted to look antique and weathered.

Materials:
1. Styrofoam ball, choice of size
2. Drinking glass to hold ball while working
3. Pearl corsage pins
4. Velvet leaves from the florist
5. Twig, in proportion to ball
6. Glue
7. Terra cotta pot
8. Small brushes
9. Acrylic paint: white, different shades of grey
10. Styrofoam to fill pot
11. Moss, from florist
12. Ribbon

Step 1. Read instructions from Velvet Artichoke (see p. 78) for covering the sphere with leaves and pins.

Step 2. After the sphere is covered with leaves, remove pin at bottom and insert twig in place. For best results, I whittle the twig into a point for easy insertion. Glue can be added to the point to ensure adhesion. Set aside to dry.

Step 3. Clean terra cotta pot to prepare for painting. Paint entire surface, including inside of the top rim with a medium-value grey. When dry, brush in a darker value of the same color. Use a small amount and scrub this darker color over the entire surface, leaving much of the original grey color showing through as shown. Do not try to create a regular pattern. Move your brush fast and irregularly to create a random effect.

Step 4. Stipple white paint irregularly over the surface with the end of your brush, creating delicate dots of paint. Again, the effect should be irregular and random to create an aged quality.

Step 5. With a stiff brush (a toothbrush can be used), spatter the darkest tone of grey randomly over the surface of the pot. This will create an antiqued effect. (When I went to a garden store to get the container for my topiary, I was unpleasantly surprised to find that decorative pots cost $35. I achieved this same look with an inexpensive terra cotta pot.)

Step 6. When pot is dry, fill container with Styrofoam to hold topiary tree in position. Insert twig into Styrofoam.

Step 7. Glue moss on Styrofoam.

Step 8. Finish off with a flurry of ribbon as shown.

A Victorian bird from Nancy's grandmother's home perches at the base of the topiary garnished with eggs and stars. Other collectibles are an assortment of nut boxes, golden buttons of clowns and moons, and steel engraved butterflies surrounded by green marbleized paper and gold gilt framing.

Bejeweled Gathering

Nancy's collection of decorative butterflies from different periods gathers in a tree of Christmas ivy.

Topiary and twig wreaths take on a special Christmas look when decorated with jewels and laden with gold.

Materials:
1. Ribbon
2. Ivy topiary
3. Decorative pins, brooches, or earrings

Step 1. Weave a piece of ribbon throughout topiary as shown.

Step 2. Decorate topiary with your own pins, brooches, and earrings.

In the background of this photograph is a Christmas baroque treatment of a classic country twig wreath.

Materials:
1. Twig wreath
2. 2″ brush
3. Quick-dry gold size varnish
4. Dutch Metal gold and copper leaf

Step 1. With a 2″ brush, spread varnish randomly over face of wreath.

Step 2. When varnish is tacky to the touch, it is ready to layer with gold and copper leaf.

Step 3. Break leaf into small, irregular pieces and let float down onto the varnished areas. Cover face of wreath in an irregular pattern, allowing the natural brown color of the twig to show through.

Step 4. With a dry brush, softly sweep away excess pieces of gold and copper leaf.

Della Robbia Beauty

In his ceramics, Della Robbia captured the beauty of nature.
Bring nature into your home with this Della Robbia tree.

An abundance of dried flora is available and so simple to use. Unique flowers, such as sunflowers and hydrangeas, can be unexpected natural elements that decorate your tree in this elegant baroque style.

Materials:
1. Christmas tree, choice of size
2. Brown paper
3. Quick-dry gold size varnish
4. Gold spray paint
5. Gold leaf
6. Newspaper
7. Florist's wire
8. Ribbon
9. Christmas mini-lights
10. Dried sunflowers and hydrangeas
11. Gold lamé fabric
12. Color Xeroxes of butterflies

Step 1. Use technique from page 72 to create antiqued brown paper to cover base of tree. I love fresh potted trees for Christmas, but always have a problem covering the pot. A quick, easy solution is to create a pouch.

Step 2. Measure the brown paper to be

sure it is at least one foot higher than your pot, to cover.

Step 3. Crush newspaper and encircle pot so that when you cover with brown paper pouch, newspaper will create the sack shape as shown in photo.

Step 4. Take lengths of crushed brown paper and fold and crease to encircle pot. Then tuck under the edge of the pot so the weight of the pot will hold brown paper in place. Encircle the pot with the brown paper. Push newspaper between pot and brown paper to create pouch effect.

Step 5. At the top of the pot, gather paper together with florist's wire, creating the top of the pouch as shown in photograph.

Step 6. Cover florist's wire with ribbon as

shown.

Step 7. Hang lights on the Christmas tree, hiding wire as much as possible down the branches of the tree.

Step 8. Place hydrangeas over entire tree to fill spaces between branches.

Step 9. Position sunflowers over entire tree. I have grouped two and three sunflowers together for strong visual impact, but use only seven in all. The main visual texture is from the hydrangeas.

Step 10. Cut lengths of gold lamé approximately 1′ by 2′. Fold into a simple knot, leaving very loose. Tuck them around the tree to balance other elements.

Step 11. Color-Xerox butterflies from books of flora or butterflies. These books can be found in libraries or bookstores. After finding the butterflies that you want to Xerox, make several copies of these images. To save cost, cut out these images and position on one 8″ × 10″ sheet. This becomes a master sheet with multiple images to be re-Xeroxed. Cut out butterflies. Wrap body of each butterfly with florist's wire and fold its wings up. Use wire to hold in place to create illusion of butterflies flying over flora in tree.

SMALL PLEASURES

In The Country Classic Style

The Country Classic Style is an evolution of the American Country look. More refined fabrics, furniture, and decorative elements are entering our country interiors. A very formal chair usually demands a formal fabric: damask, silk, or velvet. You can relax this more elegant piece with an

Garden Lane fabric from Robert Allen reproduces the floral painting of nineteenth-century botanical art.

unexpected casual play of fabric. Garden Lane, which is one of my Classic Country fabrics, is a beautiful floral print layered on top of a classic American ticking. I have upholstered this chair with a classic rope trim. The antique-finish chair takes on new life with this casual play.

This same casual but Classic Country Style is being layered into many American Country rooms, updating their rustic charm with these new elegant flourishes.

A house I de-signed in Bucks County, Pennsylvania, captures this Country Classic style. I mixed a rustic farmhouse table and a country storage chest with more formal up-holstered pieces. The sofas and chairs have been slip-covered in a casual, loose-fitting technique that sim-ply ties on to the furniture. The paintings and other decorative elements add an elegant touch.

Pillow Details

Pillows in all fabrics with different sewing details add individuality and visual texture to any seating or bedding.

The country ticking fabric is the foundation on which to layer an abundance of ideas. A pinking-sheared edge on a ruffle, or a more tailored flange will give your collection of pillows visual interest. The duffel roll pillow at far right was created simply by making a rod pocket hem and

inserting a spaghetti strap out of the same fabric, pulling it together and tying a bow, much like the classic laundry bag.

The needlepoint is a part of my Betech collection, crafted in China and inspired by a nineteenth-century watercolor in our collection of antique documents.

Garden Screen

I had artist David Comerchero create a painting of an urn in folk art style for this beautiful fire screen.

During the summer months, the fireplace, which is a charming focal point in the winter, becomes a dark, empty hole. It is so easy to dress it up with a colorful vari-

ety of fireplace decorations. Here's one I designed of a classical urn filled with a garden of flowers.

Another suggestion is a basket or urn of dried flowers. Folk art animals are also a wonderful solution.

Early twentieth-century seed-package or catalog art is a new collectible ready for framing. This example of multicolor roses from Nancy's collection is decorative, beautiful, and still inexpensive.

A special effect for ceilings can be created by using a stipple of sky blue, edged with a garland of flowers. Simply cut out a strip of the flowers from a floral wallpaper border. It's a very simple way to add a custom look to wallpapering.

Simply Elegant

Country ticking is a simple American country fabric. With an elegant hand it can be used alone to create this updated classic look.

Country ticking is the foundation of my American Country collections in fabric and wallpaper. It is an American icon that lends itself to use in many imaginative ways. I have shown you how mixing fabrics of different prints and different scales in a coordinated color story is a wonderful expressive way to give visual life to a room.

A different way to handle a space, particularly when you have interesting furniture and accessories, is to use a classic fabric as the main upholstery pattern and pepper it with interesting details.

In this corner, the wall and the slipcovered chair have been covered in ticking. The understated effect of this print is given visual interest with the sewing details. A classic slipcover is made special by adding half inch spaghetti straps to tie it in place. Instead of hidden zippers, snaps or Velcro, an elegant bow attaches the cover. The final flourish is a small pillow trimmed in an overscaled ruffle with a scalloped, pinking-sheared edge.

Certain treatments of the American Country movement are becoming more refined. Golden washes and antique silver finishes, combined with a simple print, express this country classicism. Shown here, a formal French chair has been relaxed by being slipcovered. Mirrors or art, framed in elegant golden finishes, are an ideal way to add this touch of luxury to a simple country room. Layer in fine silver and a delightful flea market find of carved fruit, as I have here.

98

Seasonal Change

During the summertime in the South, they slipcover the upholstery in a change of fabric for a fresh feeling. Here that idea receives a new twist.

When winter winds blow outside, you can bring flowers inside by transforming this simple curtain from a small stripe pattern to a large-scale floral. These pinking-sheared curtains have an elegant reversible ruffle made from a classic ticking stripe.

Step 1. The ruffle was created by doubling the fabric and sewing it into the seam.
Step 2. Pinking shears were used to cut the edge, giving the curtains this wonderful design detail.

Curtain rods with bunny motifs and rings have been sponged by artist Ivan Barnett. Country Ticking reverses to Garden Lane in this classic pleated curtain.

Enchanted Illusions

Mementos of recent trips and long-remembered friendships are enclosed in a fantasy world of stars and glowing candles.

Underneath the chipped plaster of this Finnish doll head, I can see the European newspaper used in the paper maché technique. This year, I showered this wonderful memento with a cascade of golden stars. The domes were simply layered with adhesive stars. This started a play of stars dancing over candles and crystal for a festive evening.

Beaded fruit from the antique fairs of East Hampton has become a sought-after prize.

Family Treasures

Victorian collectibles, loved teddy bears, glorious cupids,
and other family memorabilia become treasured Christmas decorations when dressed in holiday spirits.

This Christmas we used family photographs framed in nine-teenth-century silver frames as ornament for our tree. This charming frame was acquired on a trip down Por-

tobello Road in London. To finish it off, I added decorative gold berries and miniature pine cones.

For christmas fun I dress up our Gear Bears in festive holiday attire.

Christmas Vineyard

*Vineyard motifs show up throughout my work.
Here I've dressed up grapes in baroque style.*

This is a perfect example of taking an everyday object and filling it with Christmas joy. Christmas glitter has been scattered with a playful hand. Here, in order to give the ornament more of an antique quality, I worked the gold against the purple of the grape, allowing some of the purple color to show through.

Materials:
1. Newspaper
2. Plastic fruit or pine cone
3. Christmas ornament hanger
4. Spray mount
5. Tray or plate
6. Glitter
7. Decorative leaves from floral market
8. Ribbon
9. Tassel from trim store
10. Floral wire

Step 1. Cover a large area with paper to protect surface from glue.
Step 2. Fasten ornament hanger to fruit or pine cone.
Step 3. Spray fruit or pine cone with Spray Mount.
Step 4. Hold ornament over tray by hanger in one hand and sprinkle glitter on it with the other.
Step 5. Decorate with leaves, ribbon, or tassel with floral wire as shown.

106

SMALL PLEASURES

In The

Neo Traditional

Style

The Neo-Traditional Style is an opulent mix of textures, warm woods, and rich colors. Somewhat formal yet sometimes whimsical, this style often mixes antiques with new items. Traditional belongings are used in unusual ways to create gracious rooms reminiscent of bygone days, but with a more casual attitude. The overall effect is relaxed and elegant.

Rich jewel tones are the core of Neo-Traditional colors. Red in all shades is used, from burgundy to chinese lacquer to cinnabar. Greens range from deep rich hunters to soft moss tones. Browns are in hues of tobacco, sienna, and golden pecan. These colors evoke images of our past and have an antique feel about them. Warm touches of metallic gold and antique leather add variety to this rich canvas.

Drenched in deep colors, fabrics of paisleys and plaids predominate. This effect is sumptuous, a rich gathering of textures, patterns, and shapes that evoke our heritage.

Decorative pillows create a wonderful tablescape. Our collection of medals are given to descendants of the Plantagenets, the Magna Carta Dames, and the Descendants of Blood Royal.

A Golden Touch

Gilding a familiar object gives you the opportunity to rediscover it in new and inventive ways.

For the last two years, I've had great fun gilding everything from pumpkins in season to apples at Christmas to candles for parties. Once you find out how simple and fast, and how much fun it is, you may, like me, tell all your friends that if they stand still they may be gilded!

Traditionally, 24K gold gilding was used. It is still available, but expensive. What is inexpensive and readily available in art-supply stores or your local sign shop, is Dutch Metal. This material comes in packages of 25 sheets in gold, silver, or copper and is easy to apply. The fruit pictured here is plastic.

Materials:
1. Assorted plastic or wooden fruit
2. Red spray enamel, matte or shiny finish as desired. (Photo shows shiny enamel).
3. Quick-dry gold size varnish (a 4 oz. can should be enough for 50 fruits).
4. ½″ inexpensive square end brush.
5. Package Dutch Metal gold sheet (allow 1 sheet per fruit).
6. ¼″ brush.

Step 1. Spray fruit with red enamel and let dry.

Step 2. Varnish all fruit using ½″ brush. Quick-dry gold size varnish should be ready for gilding in 1 to 3 hours depending upon altitude, temperature, and humidity. The proper degree of tack should be reached before applying gilt.

Step 3. Touch varnish. It should be slightly sticky. Lift tissue of gold metal from packet of Dutch Metal. Don't be afraid of using it, the accident and imperfection of applying the gilt to the varnished surface becomes part of the antiqued finish.

Step 4. Break leaf into random-sized pieces, varying from a half inch to two inches. Notice the pieces will break with an irregular edge. This is desirable to create the varied pattern.

Step 5. Lay the broken pieces together over the surface to be gilded. A moist finger easily lifts the gold leaf for positioning. Vary the density and pattern play from fruit to fruit. Allow the red to show through as you desire. The Dutch Metal should readily adhere to the varnished surface if the varnish is at the right degree of tack. If the varnish is too wet, wait until it dries more. If it has become too dry, just re-varnish.

Step 6. After you have applied the metal to the entire surface as desired, use the dry ¼″ brush to lightly brush the gold leaf into the varnish. The gold leaf will continue to break away and will create a speckled effect in the red areas.

Step 7. Let the fruit sit until you know the varnish is dry. Lightly moisten your fingers in water and rub the fruit surface with fingertips to make sure all loose edges of gilt are rubbed into the varnish to create a smooth surface.

These look great on your Christmas tree or in large bowls as centerpieces.

A harvest of Neo-Traditional materials includes paisleys, plaids, faux wood finishes, stippled textures of burgundy and moss green. The glow of golden artifacts and the plenty of an orchard harvest are design elements that brighten your home in this warm traditional style.

Gear/Armstrong

Traditional Glow

Rich spice colors, paisley patterns, gold details, and vineyard prints create a colorful corner for dining.

The vineyard print has been brought to life by a green damask mat that brings up the green in the print. The frame is an overscaled paisley washed in gold with a thin gold inner liner separating the print

from the damask. It's hung with a simple piece of knotted rope.

Brahmin paisley wallpaper from my Neo-Traditional collection becomes a richly colored background to showcase the Brooksaw art and the Bookbinder lamps.

A lush fabric and trim treatment gives this comfortable sofa Neo-Traditional style. Most of the pillows are trimmed with a golden rope; some are knotted at the corners. The broadtail pillow bears a heraldic crest and has tassels on the corners. Over-scale fringe gives a small velvet pillow a special look.

Gear Armstrong

Crazy Quilt Patchwork

Two worlds were combined in this patchwork pattern of marbleized papers.

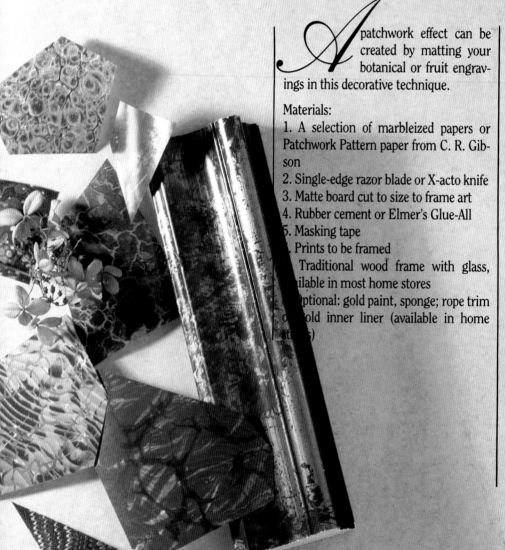

A patchwork effect can be created by matting your botanical or fruit engravings in this decorative technique.

Materials:

1. A selection of marbleized papers or Patchwork Pattern paper from C. R. Gibson
2. Single-edge razor blade or X-acto knife
3. Matte board cut to size to frame art
4. Rubber cement or Elmer's Glue-All
5. Masking tape
6. Prints to be framed
7. Traditional wood frame with glass, available in most home stores
8. Optional: gold paint, sponge; rope trim or gold inner liner (available in home stores)

Step 1. Collect an assortment of marbleized papers in harmonious colors. Cut with your X-acto knife in irregular triangular and trapezoid shapes as shown to the scale of your matte to be covered.

Step 2. Beginning at one end of your matte, glue your pieces in place. Slightly overlap your papers to be sure to cover all matte board. Work your way around matte board to cover it.

Step 3. Use matte to frame art. Remove excess paper with razor blade or X-acto knife. The edge between matte and print can be left as is but I prefer to trim it with a gold inner liner or rope. Simply tape trim to back of matte board with masking tape so that a thin edge shows in front.

Step 4. Assemble art and attach with masking-tape on back of matte.

Step 5. Insert glass and matted art into frame.

Ready-made frames come in a variety of traditional finishes. Select a warm wood tone for this look. I have created an antiqued finish by sponging gold paint over the wood.

A rich glow of burgundy and paisley gives this kitchen Neo-Traditional style. I created an elegant but intimate dining nook in what has become the entertainment area. The stove is hidden within the counter. Here, everyone can take part in cooking and serving the meal.

Gear/Armstrong

Traditional Mix

*The bedroom is a special and private world. I love to layer groups
of patterns to create a warm feeling of color for bed dressing.*

For this Neo-Traditional corner, the rich tones of wood from the Grange sleighbed form an elegant frame for our pattern mix. I usually combine a small print, in this case, the burgundy Gear ticking, with a major decorative pattern. My rich opulent paisley has been added for more texture and pattern play. Gear's classic traditional plaid in the same colors

of rich burgundy, moss green, and tea-stained brown, have completed this robust combination. A needlepoint pillow has been thrown in for whimsy.

Collectibles include paisley hearts and bears, nineteenth century cuff links, and my favorite watch with a hand-beaded band.

Velvet Touches

Traditional elegance has been added to this curtain and rod by covering the rod and lining the curtain with velvet.

In this simple curtain treatment, both the rod and the lining of the curtain are enhanced by an unexpected use of velvet. Quilting it, as I've done here, adds an interesting texture.

Most cities have quilters who will quilt your fabric for a relatively small fee. Here, in this curtain, the velvet has been quilted to itself. Another variation is to quilt the velvet lining to the curtain fabric.

I prefer to use metal rods because they will support more weight than wooden rods and do not warp. The metal rod was necessary here because of the weight of the quilted velvet lining.

Materials:
1. Velvet in desired color, yardage as needed
2. Wooden or metal curtain rod, length as needed
3. Scissors
4. Fabric glue
5. Brush, 1¼″ wide
6. Eye-screws, one per curtain loop

Step 1. Roll fabric around rod, giving yourself an extra ¼″ for overlap. Be sure to use one piece of the velvet to cover the entire length of the rod. This long length of fabric can be taken from the edge of the fabric that will be quilted later for your curtain lining. Cut fabric.

Step 2. Follow instructions of your brand of fabric glue and brush glue over entire rod.

Step 3. Lay rod on edge of fabric and roll around. If rod is very long, you may need someone to help keep fabric straight on the rod. Roll fabric around entire rod and overlap the extra ¼″. Be careful with fabric adhesive — if you use too much it will bleed over the velvet. When hanging rod, be sure to position it so the join faces the wall.

Large curtain rings have been gold-leafed in the crackle finish from page 114. Use this same process over the rings to complete this Neo-Traditional curtain treatment.

When the rings are dry screw an eye-screw onto each ring. Then sew the back of curtain to the eye-screws. The distance between loops can be varied to the amount of swag desired.

This way of covering an open storage area, whether it be shelves, a closet, or an entryway to another space, is an old idea made new. Gilded loops are shown here with our collection of antique Indian cigarette labels.

Butterfly Fantasy

*Color Xeroxes of illustrative details, such as butterflies, birds,
flowers, and architectural elements, can be decoupaged to wall paper or painted walls
for a decorative gesture.*

The color Xerox is one of the most exciting new tools for adding ornamentation throughout the home. In this enclosed entertainment bar, I added a flock of butterflies.

Materials:
1. Color Xeroxes of your chosen images. Use as many as needed to suit your project
2. Scissors
3. Elmer's Glue-All or wallpaper paste
4. Small brush
5. Wallpapered or painted wall. In this area, I have used a stipple pattern of wallpaper
6. A small piece of cardboard
7. Sponge
8. Semi-gloss clear varnish

Step 1. Xerox butterflies or other pictorial elements to be decoupaged. Combine images on one sheet of paper to save cost. They can be enlarged or reduced from original size on the Xerox to fit your project.

Step 2. Cut out images.

Step 3. Mix Elmer's Glue-All with water to a milky consistency. To the wallpaper or painted wall, glue the butterflies in place by brushing glue or paste on back of cut-out Xeroxes.

Step 4. Position butterfly on wall. With a small piece of cardboard press excess glue from behind Xerox to adhere flatly and firmly. Glue or paste will dry clear, so don't be afraid to get it on the wall. Excess can be cleaned away with a lightly moistened sponge. When design is completed, let dry.

Step 5. Add a light semi-gloss varnish to give the wall a finishing glaze if desired. Let dry. If a matte finish is desired, varnish step can be omitted.

A ceramic basket from Italy has a tri-metal coloring of pewter, copper, and gold. The framed Bacchus photograph is a memory of a visit to the Louvre.

SMALL PLEASURES

Small

Christmas

Pleasures

A Scrapbook
Of Ideas, Thoughts
& Memories

Christmas in New York draws a close to a festive year of entertaining. After the summer of friends and weekend events in East Hampton, fall activities center around our home in New York. Fall evenings of dinner parties, Halloween fun, and Thanksgiving festivities, cul-

"Merry Christmas!" is surrounded by the words "Peace, happiness, success, health, and long life." It is a Victorian sentiment, so heartwarming in these unsettled times.

minate in an enthusiastic golden Christmas season.

As fall begins, a series of decorative changes take place in our home. For small dinner parties, a few imaginative flourishes are put in place. For Halloween and Thanksgiving, seasonal elements add to the changing moods for each holiday. Just after Thanksgiving, I begin preparing for my favorite season of the year, Christmas. The lush side of my nature takes over, and I garland our trees with boxwood, hydrangeas, and swags of gold and copper lamé.

I love to be playful and follow my emotions. Gold gilding makes almost anything have a Christmas Spirit. The secret is not to worry if it crackles or is uneven—it only adds to the antique patina. Gold and copper touches are sprinkled like snow. Candlelight fills our home with its warm glow and good cheer.

Christmas fills me with warm memories. A cornucopia of golden fruit, a swirl of gold lamé, the glitter of beaded ornaments, the flurry of decorative butterflies, and the glow of a radiant sun combine in this most festive season.

M any of the decorative ideas that I use throughout the year are invented in this season. It's a time when I love to experiment with new combinations of materials and ideas. Adding to last year's decorations brings new richness and depth.

I hope you enjoy making some of these decorations. Your family and friends can join in. Create your own wonderful events for all to remember and cherish in this glowing Baroque Christmas Style.

*M*y collection of cupids fills me with Christmas joy. Plaster castings have been gilded and antiqued. I use them throughout the home in table settings and decorative Christmas displays.

*A*glow with a Christmas forest of candle-light, our buffet for Christ-mas Eve is a holiday festi-val. Our collection of candelabra envelops the area with a warm joyful spirit. Trees are garlanded and wrapped with swirls of gold.

Christmas Garden

*Garden sculptures can come indoors for the holidays. I entwined
this charming sculpture with a garland of hydrangeas, roses, and butterflies.*

To create a Victorian Christmas garden for our buffet, a group of small trees was decorated and gathered together with this garlanded garden sculpture.

Materials:
1. Dried hydrangeas
2. Florist's wire
3. Christmas berries
4. Silk and dried roses
5. Xeroxed butterflies (see p. 128)

Step 1. After the major trees have been decorated (see p. 138) with the full blooms of dried hydrangeas, small broken pieces of the blossoms remain. A perfect way to use these fragments of dried flowers is to create small, delicate garlands. Simply roll out florist's wire to the length you desire and thread hydrangeas on the wire.

Step 2. After this garland of hydrangeas is created, tie off both ends in place so that other elements can be added. With florist's wire, simply arrange the other decorative pieces and secure with wire. Position your color Xeroxed butterflies so that they are flying around this beautiful floral piece.

Our collection of nineteenth-century candelabra fills the buffet with the warm glow of Christmas light.

Velvet Treasures

*Rich textures combine to create a simple, but dramatic
decoration for this new burst of Christmas baroque.*

The last two Christmases, I made velvet fabric balls. The technique is so simple and fast that in one afternoon, I made 50.

Materials:
1. An 18″ square of velvet
2. Crushed newspaper
3. Florist's wire
4. Gold ribbon
5. Golden leaves or glass ornaments

Step 1. Lay velvet square on table. Crush a ball of newspaper to size of ornament desired. Place ball in center of square.

Step 2. Fold over four edges of velvet to conceal ragged edges of fabric when ornament is completed.

Step 3. Wrap velvet around ball of crushed newspaper and tie with florist's wire at top to create a pouch.

Step 4. Tie a ribbon bow around neck of pouch for decoration.

Step 5. Add a garnish of golden grapes as shown here or other Christmas berries, silk roses, or velvet leaves.

Candle's Glow

*The glow of a simple candle becomes grand when scattered over
a reflective tray of golden gilt.*

I created this tray from a $15 flea market find. It had been a metal Tole tray in an earlier life. Discarded and rusted, it was given a new life and a coat of gold.

Materials:

1. An inexpensive metal tray or platter, perhaps a flea-market find.
2. Quick-dry gold size varnish
3. 1½" square-end brush
4. ¼" brush
5. Optional spray paint, your choice of color

Step 1. Clean tray or platter.

Step 2. Varnish with the quick-dry varnish if you want the coloration of your tray to show through. If not, create your own base coat of color by spray painting your tray or platter with the color you desire.

Step 3. When the varnish is tacky to the touch, it is ready to receive gold leaf. Follow instructions on page 114 for gold leafing.

A Victorian Christmas gift of a cat pin cushion is wrapped in a nineteenth century decorative box.

Swirl of Gold

The fastest Christmas tree that I did this year in the grand baroque style is just a swirl of gold and copper lamé.

For a simple yet elegant Christmas tree, weave a lattice of gold and copper lamé through its boughs. It's fast and simple, but creates an opulent visual display.

Materials:

1. Christmas tree
2. Tiny Christmas lights
3. Dried hydrangeas
4. Gold and copper lamé
5. Plastic ivy painted gold (see p. 38)
6. Golden glass ornaments

Step 1. Cover tree with miniature lights, hiding wires by wrapping around stems.

Step 2. Tuck dried hydrangeas into spaces between tree branches.

Step 3. Intertwine 6″ strips of gold and copper lamé around the tree as shown. For best effect, I crush lamé into a small ball to give the fabric a more antique quality.

Step 4. Add branches of golden ivy.

Step 5. Add a few golden glass pears for the final touch.

Golden glass ornaments, nineteenth century Victorian birds, and gilded fruits add Christmas beauty to this simple tree.

Green Garlands

At Christmas, small corners are given a special seasonal flourish.
Here, a painting is dressed up in Christmas greens.

This elegant garland is a simple addition that can give a nook, wall, or painting, the holiday spirit.

Materials:
1. Boxwood garland from your Christmas shop or florist supplier
2. Florist's wire
3. Christmas berries and pine cones
4. Glass and glitter Christmas decorations
5. Ribbon

Step 1. Position garland around three sides of painting. Hold in place by wire.
Step 2. At top of painting, create a focal point. In this design I used Christmas berries and small pine cones.
Step 3. Randomly place glass and glitter ornaments as shown.
Step 4. At the top corners, add a bow.

At Christmas time, our home is adorned with Nancy's collection of Victorian Christmas memorabilia, here unexpectedly tucked in the corner of a traditional painting. At left, traditional glass balls are wrapped in ribbon. Add velvet leaves for decorative detail.

Simple Pleasures

At Christmas, simple embellishments are added throughout our home to decorative pieces that are on display all year long.

collection of beaded fruit has been scattered on shelves with my service of pitchers. The country style is represented by the simple terra cotta country pitchers on the middle shelf. Below are two repoussé examples of nineteenth-century silver craft. Above them are reproductions from Hall China of a traditional ce-

ramic form washed in a coat of gold. For this season, clusters of Christmas berries and tiny pine cones were added to each pitcher's handle. Nineteenth-century pressed metal birds from the flea markets of Paris perch beside an antique curtain pull, twisted into a cuff of gold.

Christmas Eve in our New York home is a time that Nancy and I share with friends both old and new. Our table is set around a Christmas orchard. A tablescape of golden angels, glowing candles, and Christmas place settings welcome friends in this most special time.

Christmas Orchard

A Della Robbia orchard was created for our Christmas table. You can achieve the same effect by using the techniques you have learned throughout this book. Faux and dried flowers and fruit, painted ivy, and color Xeroxes can help you create a baroque still life for the holidays.

Our Christmas orchard became the centerpiece for Christmas Eve dining. Arranged in a classical urn of grand scale was a traditional spruce Christmas tree.

Materials:
1. Spruce tree
2. Tiny Christmas lights
3. Dried hydrangeas
4. Red berries
5. Gold painted ivy (see page 38)
6. Faux plums
7. Dried pomegranates
8. Silk and dried roses
9. Color Xeroxed butterflies
10. Golden decorative ornaments

Step 1. Illuminate the tree with the tiniest of Christmas lights.

Step 2. Cover with an abundance of dried hydrangeas.

Step 3. Rope garlands of red berries with long twigs around the tree.

Step 4. Add golden painted ivy.

Step 5. Scatter faux plums and dried pomegranates throughout.

Step 6. Add silk roses, made from ribbons and simply twisted into bud-like shapes. Add dried roses.

Step 7. Place butterflies from color Xeroxes on the tree.

Step 8. Add large, golden decorative curtain-pulls.

Beautiful baroque curtain pulls were found in an East Hampton antique fair.

Festive Greetings

Christmas Eve is our time to share with friends and family.
Candlelight washes the table in golden splendor.

etting the table for Christmas Eve festivities is one of the season's best treats. Heralding angels greet each friend. Oversized golden chargers await the first course. Lavish red damask napkins and table gifts of crackled fruit with butterflies perched in anticipation com-

plete the look. The first toast of the evening from a goblet richly cuffed with gold begins this year's celebration.

As a Christmas present for Nancy, I had these vintage forks gilded in a wash of gold. Each is a different baroque pattern.

$\mathcal{A}$s we look towards the future, we also look back to shared memories of good times. By giving form to our own visual and personal fantasies, we embellish our everyday world with excitement and pleasure. I hope my book has taught you to use your own collections, your own memories, and your own talents to make these simple pleasures a grand and glorious part of your future.

With
Warmest Feelings
And Shared
Love,

Raymond Waites.